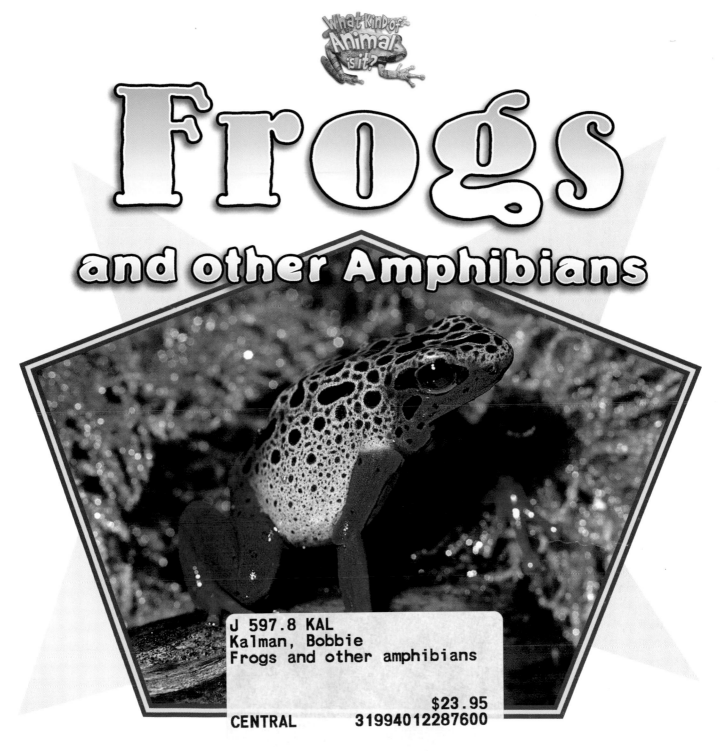

What Kind of Animal is it?

Frogs
and other Amphibians

Bobbie Kalman
Crabtree Publishing Company
www.crabtreebooks.com

Frogs
and other Amphibians

Created by Bobbie Kalman

Dedicated by Bobbie and Peter
For our new grandson Charlie, who never ceases to amaze us.
We love you so much!

Editor-in-Chief
Bobbie Kalman

Writing team
Bobbie Kalman
Reagan Miller
Kathryn Smithyman

Substantive editor
Kelley MacAulay

Editors
Molly Aloian
Robin Johnson

Design
Katherine Kantor
Robert MacGregor (series logo)

Production coordinator
Katherine Kantor

Photo research
Crystal Foxton

Consultant
Patricia Loesche, Ph.D., Animal Behavior Program,
Department of Psychology, University of Washington

Illustrations
Barbara Bedell: pages 5 (mudpuppy), 8, 14 (top-left and right),
    18 (top left and right, and slug), 26, 31 (middle), 32 (frog, habitats,
    mudpuppy, and newt)
Katherine Kantor: pages 10 (middle left), 14 (middle left), 18 (mosquito),
    32 (lungs and vertebrates)
Margaret Amy Reiach: pages 16 (top-left and right), 18 (spider), 31 (bottom)
Bonna Rouse: pages 4, 5 (all except mudpuppy), 7 (right), 12,
    16 (bottom-left and right), 17, 18 (earthworm), 23, 27, 28, 30 (bottom),
    32 (caecilian, salamander, siren, and toad)
Tiffany Wybouw: pages 7 (left), 9, 10 (top left and right), 20, 22, 24,
    30 (top-left and right)

Photographs
Bruce Coleman, Inc.: Jack Dermid: page 27 (bottom); Kim Taylor: page 19
AbleStock/Index Stock: page 27 (top right)
© Dwight Kuhn: page 13 (bottom)
Robert McCaw: page 13 (top)
Minden Pictures: Michael & Patricia Fogden: page 29
Photo Researchers, Inc.: Stephen Dalton: pages 18, 22 (bottom left);
    Mark Smith: page 11 (bottom)
Other images by Corel and Digital Vision

Crabtree Publishing Company

www.crabtreebooks.com   1-800-387-7650

Copyright © 2005 CRABTREE PUBLISHING COMPANY.
All rights reserved. No part of this publication may be
reproduced, stored in a retrieval system or be transmitted in
any form or by any means, electronic, mechanical, photocopying,
recording, or otherwise, without the prior written permission
of Crabtree Publishing Company. In Canada: We acknowledge the
financial support of the Government of Canada through the Book
Publishing Industry Development Program (BPIDP) for our
publishing activities.

Cataloging-in-Publication Data
Kalman, Bobbie.
  Frogs and other amphibians / Bobbie Kalman.
    p. cm. -- (What kind of animal is it?)
  Includes index.
  ISBN-13: 978-0-7787-2159-8 (RLB)
  ISBN-10: 0-7787-2159-0 (RLB)
  ISBN-13: 978-0-7787-2217-5 (pbk.)
  ISBN-10: 0-7787-2217-1 (pbk.)
  1. Frogs--Juvenile literature. 2. Amphibians--Juvenile literature. I. Title.
II. Series.
  QL668.E2K339 2005
  597.8--dc22
                                                    2005000497
                                                    LC

**Published in
the United States**
PMB16A
350 Fifth Ave.
Suite 3308
New York, NY
10118

**Published
in Canada**
616 Welland Ave.,
St. Catharines, Ontario
Canada
L2M 5V6

**Published in the
United Kingdom**
73 Lime Walk
Headington
Oxford
OX3 7AD
United Kingdom

**Published
in Australia**
386 Mt. Alexander Rd.,
Ascot Vale (Melbourne)
VIC 3032

Contents

What are amphibians?

poison dart frog

Amphibians are animals. There are many kinds of amphibians! Amphibians belong to three groups. The groups are shown on these pages.

Frogs and toads

Frogs and toads make up the largest group of amphibians. These animals do not have tails.

cane toad

caecilian

Caecilians

Caecilians have long, thin bodies. They make up another group of amphibians.

siren

Salamanders

Amphibians that have tails are called **salamanders**. Sirens, salamanders, newts, and mudpuppies make up this group of amphibians.

salamander

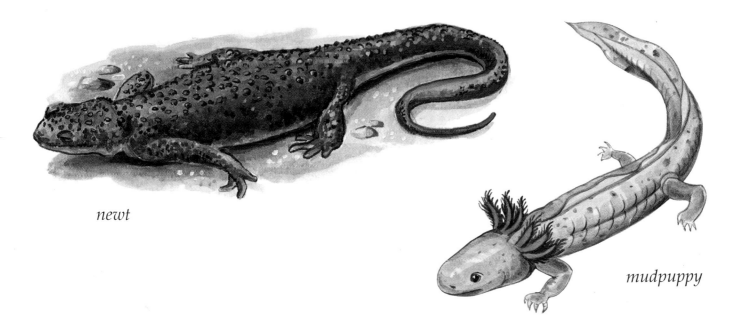

newt

mudpuppy

In water and on land

The word "amphibian" means "two lives." The lives of amphibians have two parts. The first part is spent in water. Amphibians live in water when they are young. When they are fully grown, amphibians spend the second part of their lives mainly on land.

When it was young, this salamander lived in a pond or a river. The salamander is fully grown now, and it lives on land.

Two habitats

Amphibians live in two **habitats** during their lives. A habitat is the natural place where an animal lives. Young amphibians live in water habitats such as ponds, swamps, and lakes. Fully grown amphibians live in land habitats such as forests that are near water.

A bullfrog lives at the edge of a lake or a pond. It spends some time in water and some time on land.

Cold-blooded animals

Amphibians are **cold-blooded** animals.
The body temperature of a cold-blooded
animal is the same temperature as the place
where it lives. When the weather is cold, an
amphibian's body is cold. When the weather
is warm, an amphibian's body is warm.

Some amphibians live in warm places, and others live in cold places.
This tree frog lives in South America, where the weather is warm.

Hot and cold

When an amphibian gets too hot, it needs to cool off its body. To cool off, it jumps into water or sits in the shade. When an amphibian gets too cold, it needs to warm up its body. It may sit in the sun to warm itself.

The salamander shown above is warming itself in the sun. This frog is jumping into water to cool off.

Amphibian bodies

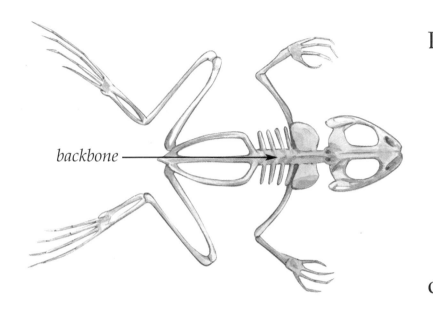

backbone

Different amphibians have different bodies. All amphibians have **backbones** inside their bodies, however. A backbone is a group of bones in the middle of an animal's back.

Frogs and toads

Frogs and toads have small, round bodies.

Most frogs and toads have big eyes near the top of their heads.

Frogs and toads have four legs. Frogs have long back legs. Toads have short back legs.

10

Salamanders

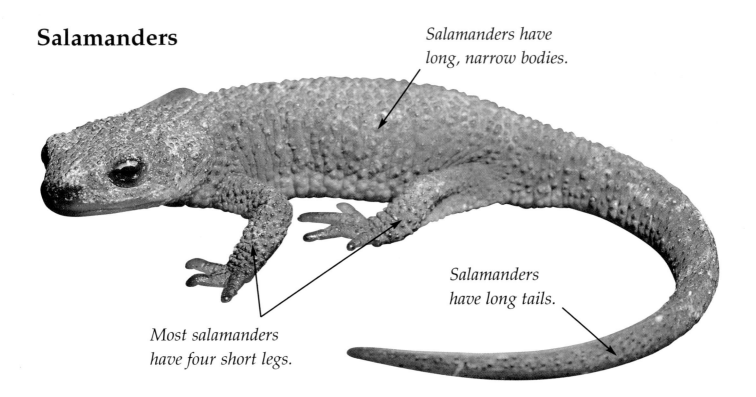

Salamanders have long, narrow bodies.

Salamanders have long tails.

Most salamanders have four short legs.

Caecilians

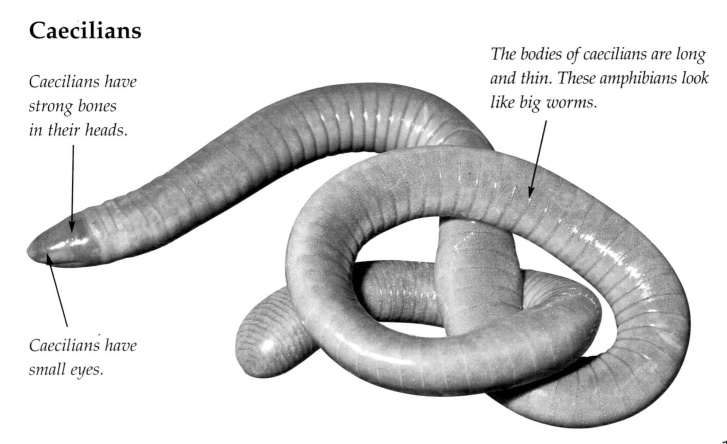

Caecilians have strong bones in their heads.

The bodies of caecilians are long and thin. These amphibians look like big worms.

Caecilians have small eyes.

On the move!

Amphibians can move quickly on land. Frogs have strong back legs. They use their back legs to take long leaps through the air. Salamanders use their short legs to walk or to run. Caecilians **slither**. To slither means to slide on the belly.

A salamander walks slowly, but it runs when it is in danger.

Good swimmers

Most amphibians move easily in water. Frogs swim by kicking their back legs. Caecilians and some kinds of salamanders swim by moving their long tails from side to side. Other salamanders walk on the bottoms of ponds or lakes.

After a long swim, a frog sometimes rests on a lily pad.

Webbed feet

Some frogs spend most of their lives in water. These kinds of frogs have **webbed feet**. Webbed feet have skin between the toes. Having webbed feet helps frogs swim quickly through water.

Breathing air

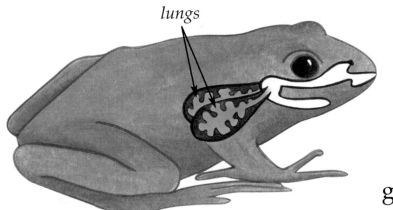

lungs

Lungs are body parts that take in air. They also let out air.

All amphibians must breathe **oxygen** to stay alive. Oxygen is a gas that is in air. Oxygen is also in water. Most fully grown amphibians breathe air using **lungs**. Lungs are inside an animal's body.

Frogs cannot use their lungs to breathe under water.
They have to come out of the water to breathe air.

Special skin

Most amphibians breathe using lungs, but they also breathe through their skin! An amphibian's skin is covered with **pores**. Pores are tiny holes. Oxygen comes into an amphibian's body through its pores. Some amphibians have no lungs. They breathe only through their pores.

This salamander does not have lungs. It breathes through the pores in its skin.

Slippery skin

An amphibian cannot take in oxygen through dry skin. Its skin must be wet. An amphibian's skin is covered with **mucus**. Mucus is slime. It keeps an amphibian's skin wet. Mucus makes a frog's skin look shiny.

Finding food

earthworm

spider

Adult amphibians are **predators**. Predators are animals that hunt other animals for food. The animals that predators eat are called **prey**. Amphibians eat many kinds of prey. They eat slugs, earthworms, and spiders. They also eat insects such as flies and mosquitoes.

mosquito

slug

Large amphibians can eat prey as big as mice! This horned frog is eating a mouse.

Catching food

Most frogs and salamanders have long, sticky tongues. They use their tongues to catch prey. When a frog sees an insect, it flicks its tongue out of its mouth. The insect sticks to the frog's tongue. The frog then pulls its tongue back into its mouth and eats the insect.

This frog is using its long tongue to catch a damselfly.

Staying safe

This frog is green, just like the leaf. Its color may hide the frog from predators.

Many predators eat amphibians. Amphibians hide from predators in different ways. Many amphibians have skin colors that match colors in their habitats. Having matching colors makes it hard to see these amphibians. Other amphibians come out only at night, when it is easier to hide from predators.

Most salamanders hide in logs or under rocks during the day. They come out only at night.

Bright colors

Some amphibians have poison in their skin. Poison makes them taste terrible to predators. Amphibians that have poison do not need to hide from their predators. Instead, they have brightly colored skin that can be seen easily. Most predators stay away from amphibians that have brightly colored skin.

This California newt has poison in its skin. The poison in the newt's body is so strong that it can kill large snakes and birds!

These blue poison dart frogs do not need to hide during the day. Their bright color warns predators to stay away!

Frogs and toads

The common reed frog is one of the smallest frogs in the world.

Most amphibians are frogs or toads. There are thousands of kinds of frogs and toads! Some are large, and others are small. Some have brightly colored skin. Others are dull brown or green. Do you know how frogs and toads are different? If not, find out on the next page!

Most kinds of poison dart frogs are bright red, orange, or yellow.

The oriental fire-bellied toad has black and bright-red markings on its belly.

The tomato frog's skin is as red as a tomato!

Frog or toad?

Sometimes it is hard to tell if an amphibian is a frog or a toad. Read the chart below to learn about the differences between some kinds of frogs and toads.

frog

toad

Frogs

- Frogs have smooth skin.
- Frogs have wet skin.
- Frogs have long back legs.
- Frogs are good jumpers.

Toads

- Toads have bumpy skin.
- The skin of toads is drier than the skin of frogs.
- The back legs of toads are shorter than the back legs of frogs.
- Instead of jumping, toads usually walk.

Tree frogs

Some frogs spend their lives in trees. Frogs that live in trees are called **tree frogs**. Tree frogs are great climbers! A few kinds of tree frogs do not live in trees all the time. They sometimes live in tall grass on the ground.

Most tree frogs have small, light bodies. Their small bodies help them balance on the branches and leaves of trees.

Sticky toes

Tree frogs have sticky pads on their toes. Sticky pads help tree frogs hold on to branches and leaves as they climb trees. Both of the red-eyed tree frogs on this page are hanging on by their toes!

sticky pad

Tree frogs spread their toes apart to help them hold on to branches.

Salamanders

Salamanders, newts, sirens, and mudpuppies make up the salamander group of amphibians. Newts and salamanders start their lives in water. Many live on land when they are adults, just as other amphibians do. Other newts and salamanders never leave the water!

Many of the salamanders that live on land live in forests. They hunt slow-moving animals such as earthworms and snails. This spotted salamander is hunting an earthworm.

Life in the water

Sirens and mudpuppies spend their whole lives in water. They breathe using gills. Sirens and mudpuppies hunt small fish and insects.

A mudpuppy breathes using gills. Its gills are on the outside of its body.

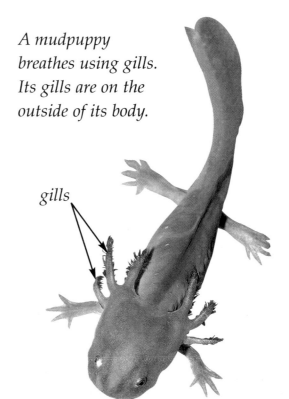

gills

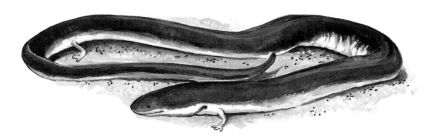

This salamander lives under water, even when it is an adult. It is called a three-toed amphiuma.

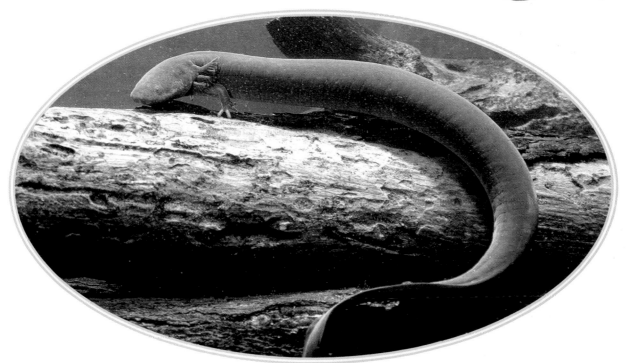

A siren has small front legs and no back legs.

 # Caecilians

Most caecilians live in warm places. Many live in underground homes called **burrows**. Caecilians sometimes come above the ground after it rains. They lie in puddles and take in water through their pores. A few kinds of caecilians live in water all the time.

Finding their way

Most caecilians do not see well. They have small eyes. They live under the ground, where it is dark. Caecilians sometimes use two feelers to find their way around. The feelers may also help caecilians smell.

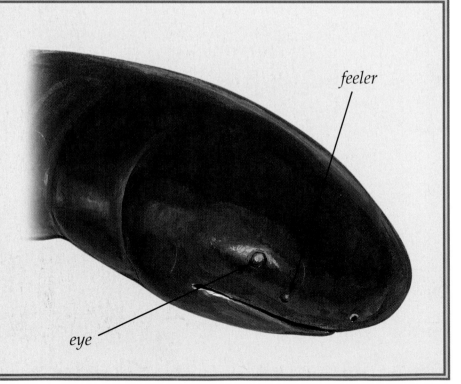

feeler

eye

Most caecilians are below the ground a lot of the time. People do not see them very often.

🐸 Guess who? 🐸

In this book, you have learned a lot
about frogs and other amphibians.
Now it is time to test yourself! Read
the riddles below and use what you
have learned to solve them.

Riddle #1

We are part of the frog group,
and our skin has bumps.
Our back legs are short,
and we rarely jump!
(Turn to page 23 for a clue.)

Riddle #2

We look a lot like newts.
We hunt earthworms and snails.
We often move slowly
and have very long tails.
(Need a hint? Turn to page 26.)

Super solving!

You are doing very well! Read on to solve more riddles. The answers to the riddles are at the bottom of this page.

Riddle #3

We live in trees
and we climb them like pros.
We grab on to branches
with our sticky toes.
(Read pages 24-25 for clues.)

Riddle #4

We live under the ground,
and have very small eyes.
If you guess who we are,
you are certainly wise!
(Turn to pages 28-29 for clues.)

Answers:
1. Toads
2. Salamanders
3. Tree frogs
4. Caecilians

Words to know and Index

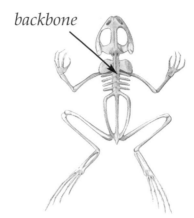

backbone

backbone
page 10

caecilians
pages 4, 11, 12, 13, 28-29, 31

frogs
pages 4, 7, 8,
9, 10, 12, 13,
14, 15, 16-17,
18, 19, 20, 21,
22-25, 30, 31

gills

gills
pages 16, 27

pond

habitats
pages 7, 20

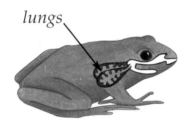

lungs

lungs
pages 14, 15, 16, 17

mudpuppies
pages 5, 26, 27

newts
pages 5, 21, 26, 30

salamanders
pages 5, 6, 9, 11, 12, 13,
15, 19, 20, 26, 27, 31

sirens
pages 5, 26, 27

toads
pages 4, 10, 22-23, 31

1 2 3 4 5 6 7 8 9 0   Printed in the U.S.A.   4 3 2 1 0 9 8 7 6 5